The Old Men Will Die First
A True Story of

Cold War Espionage

Peter F. MacDoran

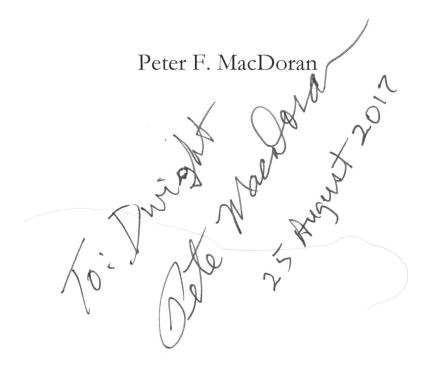

ISBN: 1530749042
ISBN-13: 9781530749041

DEDICATION

Dr. William H. Pickering (1919–2004), former Director of the
NASA/Caltech, Jet Propulsion Laboratory (JPL) for 22 years, a quiet man
of truly extraordinary leadership skills with whom I had occasional contact
during my eight overlapping years at JPL. His selection of me to join him in
the USSR in October 1973 was initially a high honor, devolving into events
that put my life at risk. I now understand what necessitated that risk—
a matter of global survival.

CONTENTS

Part 1

Baku, Azerbaijan Republic, USSR—October 9, 1973, mid-morning

An imposing, athletic, maybe seven-foot tall Soviet man strode into the international scientific conference. Word quietly spread among the delegates from the US and western countries that this man was a KGB officer and that other KGB were likely also there.

Suddenly approaching me (a member of the American delegation), and without any introduction, the officer snapped, "Are you one of the Capitalists?"

"I am an American, so I suppose that makes me a Capitalist."

He bent to look me in the eyes. "Do you know the difference between Capitalism and Communism?"

"I believe I do, but it is likely not the same as your understanding of it."

"No, you and I have the same understanding. In the Capitalist world, man exploits man, but here in the Communist world, it is the other way around." His laughter boomed at his own joke. Then, abruptly, he stopped and became deadly serious.

"Do you realize that the most humane invention ever made by man is the invention of nuclear weapons?" His eyes bored through me with intensity.

"How can you possibly believe that?"

"Throughout all of human history there have been old men who were safely on the mountain tops who ordered large numbers of young men onto the field of battle to fight and probably die, but…in the next global war, it will be the old men who will die first. " The KGB officer turned abruptly and walked away. I was stunned but have never forgotten his words.

[**About the Title**: Every modern military compiles the organizational structure of its adversaries. In the modern parlance, it is summed up in the abbreviation C5ISR which will be targeted for initial massive nuclear attacks. Those initials stand for Command, Control, Communications, Computing, Combat Systems, Intelligence, Surveillance, and Reconnaissance. It is the old men who command the C5ISR infrastructures and those war fighting capabilities will be the first to be eradicated. In the age of nuclear warfare, there is no such thing as the safety of the "mountain tops" and the collateral damage to the planet and all that inhabit it, will be truly inestimable.]

"If This Middle East War Becomes Worse, You will be Arrested."

JPL scientist, Dr. Richard Davies, was invited by the Soviet scientific organizers of this XXIV International Astronautical Congress in Baku because of his joint research with Soviet scientists involved in the theoretical study of gravitation. In my case, I was honored to realize that I was the only space scientist to be selected directly by Dr. William Pickering, Director of the NASA / Caltech Jet Propulsion Laboratory, to accompany him to this conference. I was 32 years old and the youngest technical presenter at the conference and without any prior contact with the USSR.

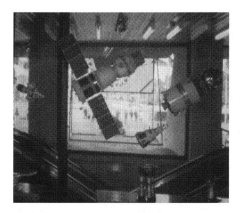

XXIV International Astronautical Congress

Official Soviet Exhibit of scale model spacecraft
V. I. Lenin Palace (35 Kirov Prospect, Baku)

I recalled Dick Davies commenting that the Soviet scientist, Dr. Igor Speranski, (not his actual name) was a Communist Party official from Moscow and a personal friend of Dr. Pickering.

[**Unknown to me at the time.** Dr. Speranski was also a close associate of Dr. Andrei Sakharov, the most prominent dissident of the Soviet Era who became the recipient of the 1975 Nobel Peace Prize. These two men, and many other dissidents, were frightened that the secretly supplied modern Soviet weapon transfers and training of Middle East militaries were leading to a US/USSR global war. On October 6th, the Yom Kippur War, AKA the 1973 Arab-Israeli War began with simultaneous attacks by Egypt and Syria against Israel. It was a perilous time for the world though most people were not aware of that.]

On the afternoon of October 9th, Dr. Speranski came to talk with me at a stand-up food court in the conference venue of the V.I. Lenin Palace. Six men, who I supposed were his security detail, quickly established a protected zone around the two of us.

"Your Dr. Pickering said I should talk to you," Speranski said after a quick introduction. "Are you aware of what is happening in the Middle East?" I answered that I'd had no news for a few days, but it seemed near war conditions. I thought, at that time, events were moving toward another Arab/Israeli war similar to the 1967 conflict.

"If this Middle East war becomes much worse, the KGB will arrest you...and KGB is already at this meeting. However, before they can arrest you, my staff and I will get you out of the country. I will need to know where you are going to be." With surprise and some misgivings at the turn of events, I handed my travel itinerary to him. He made notes and then returned my documents. The mention of KGB having any interest in me was a real concern. I wondered what could possibly be a basis for my arrest. Why just me and not all the Americans at the meeting?

All I could think to say was "thank you" to this man with the six-person security detail surrounding us, the man who was offering to prevent the KGB from arresting me. This was a really depressing conversation.

[Tel Aviv, Israel: Arab military forces, now armed with modern Soviet weapons, inflicted severe Israeli battlefield losses within the first few days of the war. Israeli military leadership feared Israel was about to be overrun. General Moshe Dayan tells President Golda Meir, "This is the end of the Third Temple." President Meir orders the arming of the Israeli nuclear weapons, code named Samson. Jewish Holy Scriptures describe the destruction of the Second Temple in 70 CE (Current Era or Common Era) by the Roman Army. Religious Jews have long planned to build a Third Temple; however, if Israel was overrun, all hope of a Third Temple would be lost.]

Former Luftwaffe Pilot Expects to be Arrested

Dr. Josef von Ulrich (not his actual name), a space scientist at the NASA Goddard Space Flight Center (GSFC) located in Greenbelt Maryland, also attended the IAF conference. About midnight on October 9th, he telephoned my room at the Intourist Hotel Baku where all we foreign conference attendees were housed. When I answered my room phone, all I initially heard was deafeningly loud music (from the one-channel music box in each hotel room). I could barely hear Josef over the din and asked him to lower the volume, which he said he could not do—he'd explain later. Josef told me to come to his hotel room as soon as I was able and gave me his room number.

When I arrived, the music was still earsplitting as he opened the door and gestured for me to take a seat. He had a bottle of vodka open and apparently had been drinking. He offered me a drink, but I declined. Pulling a chair close to me, he confided that the loud music was because all the hotel rooms were bugged.

Josef had been a Messerschmitt 109 Luftwaffe fighter/bomber pilot during World War II, a fact I thought I had heard. What most people did not know was that, beginning in 1941, he had been involved in the Siege of Leningrad that lasted two and a half years. Under Soviet law, any German combatants, especially those of the Luftwaffe, who were a part of the siege were regarded as war criminals and lifetime arrest warrants existed for any such persons. The Soviets claimed that the Siege of

Leningrad had caused the deaths of one million people.

Josef also told me that the KGB was already at our meeting, which I admitted I had recently been told. Josef expected to be arrested at any time, and he wanted me to know that, in the event he suddenly went missing, the KGB was responsible. As Josef described his fears of arrest and possible prosecution as a war criminal, it seemed reasonable to wonder why he had decided to attend this meeting in the USSR in the first place. Though, I supposed I knew why. I'd noticed in prior NASA Headquarters meetings, Josef was quite a NASA-politically attuned person, and this IAF meeting was highly prestigious.

Still, I could not understand why he'd run the risk. At an earlier NASA HQ meeting, I learned that Josef had survived World War II as a combat pilot, had been involved in the Battle of the Bulge in 1944, had been wounded, captured by US Forces, imprisoned as a POW in the Continental US, and at war's end, had been allowed to remain in the US and become a citizen. He earned technical degrees from US universities, and he progressed in US Government Service, becoming a NASA official at GSFC...and now to risk all that by getting arrested in the USSR? Pure hubris, I supposed, but, great, another reason to be concerned about the ever threatening KGB.

A phrase from my junior high school literary past, *Mad Magazine*, popped into my head, "What Me Worry?"

Pickering under Suspicion

KGB counter-intelligence suspected Dr. Pickering of being involved in a developing espionage event…to be perpetrated by unknown Soviet dissidents. For that reason, his room and luggage were searched (on 10/12). Though no espionage material was found, Pickering was ordered out of the USSR. With Pickering gone, KGB counter-intelligence focused on Davies, likely because of his prior involvements with Soviet scientists which resulted in putting him under surveillance at the conclusion of the conference.

However, the dissidents had a backup plan that involved me. Although I had not been informed that such a contingency might arise…or trained in how to deal with anything like that.

October 13th, the last day of the conference: Unknown to me at the time of the group photo session at 8:30 am, Pickering believed his hotel room and luggage had been searched while he and his wife had dined the previous evening, and he had told Davies about that.

Only the KGB would have the capability…and authority to conduct searches. Neither Pickering nor Davies mentioned to me the suspected room and luggage searches. In retrospect, I see that these events were a critical tightening of the noose restricting both of them from completing crucial plans.

"Whatever Speranski has for me, bring it to Pasadena."

At the conclusion of the official photo session of conference attendees, Dr. Pickering came up behind me and began speaking as the two of us maneuvered our way through the folding chairs.

Pickering spoke quickly and softly while not directly facing me. He said Speranski had promised to give him "something," but that he had made similar promises of "something" before and nothing ever had come of it. Pickering said he and his wife had to leave Baku soon and that Speranski had been directed to give the "something" to me.

"Whatever Dr. Speranski gives you, bring it to me in Pasadena."

I gave a quiet affirmative response while looking at the ground as both of us departed in different directions. It seemed eerily like a scene from an espionage movie. I was, of course, curious about what Speranski had intended to give to Pickering, and I assumed the "something" must be important, considering the manner in which I had been instructed to accept anything offered by the man.

"Give this to your Dr. Pickering."

A couple of hours after the photo session, Speranski, with his entourage, located me and asked me if I had a briefcase. I said yes.

"Bring it and meet me in the main conference center at fourteen hundred."

At the appointed time and place, Speranski and his security detail again set up a secure perimeter away from the view of the people packing up the many exhibits in the V.I. Lenin conference hall.

"Open your briefcase," Speranski instructed me. Then he placed a large thick unsealed business size brown envelope in it, and instructed me to close the briefcase.

"Give this to your Dr. Pickering. You must now slowly count to one hundred before you leave this place." Without any further conversation, Speranski nodded to the closest security man who nodded to the men at the outer security perimeter, and all seven of them quickly walked away. I never saw any of them again.

I'm in Serious Trouble, if Caught.

Alone in my hotel room, I was anxious to discover what was in the large unsealed envelope placed in my briefcase under such suspicious circumstances.

On initial viewing, the contents appeared to be ordinary handout materials from the conference. But then, I became alarmed. Included were some very thin lightweight papers, as might be used in airmail postage service. On them was Russian language (Cyrillic) typewriter text and crude clandestine appearing photographs of a missile weapon system. These were certainly not ordinary handouts. Being caught with such material during an expected search when attempting to leave the USSR, if similar to the thorough search I had experienced upon entering the country, would surely lead to my arrest and interrogation of how I came to have such material.

A memory of being eight years old and playing tag on the front lawn at my grandparents' home made me realize I had just been tagged and was now "it." I also remembered my grandfather, a self-taught engineer, telling me as a youngster to go to college and learn about science and engineering…so I could "help people." As a youngster, I believed his words meant that when I was big and I knew a lot of things I could "help people"…by fixing things that were broken—like the strained relationship between the US and USSR was at that time. With cold chills running up my spine, I considered destroying the large envelope and its contents, but I had no means to do so.

Not a smoker, I had no convenient fire source, and besides, smoke and/or flames would be sure to bring unwanted attention. I considered tearing up the documents and flushing the pieces down the toilet. But I immediately realized the likely result of that would be clogging the hotel plumbing—none too reliable in the first place.

All I knew for sure was that I was halfway around the world from home, in a country…sworn enemy of the United States…and that I was seemingly without any allies to help me get back home to my family or to deliver the important message to Dr. Pickering. Alone and terrified, I spent that evening, numb with misgivings, bereft of hope.

Part 2

Moscow hotel

It was about 2 am (10/14), and I was still having trouble sleeping. I began to assemble the chain of events that had gotten me into this dangerous situation. I recalled my excitement at receiving a letter from JPL making a job offer to me. The job offer letter came with a brief history of the Lab booklet. I remembered the item of October 4, 1957, the dawn of the space age when the Soviet Union had beat the US into space.

A quote from Dr. Pickering: "It was only the beeping reality of Sputnik that suddenly made the threat of intercontinental atomic warfare with ballistic rockets more than a science fiction story." Sixteen years after the beginning of the space age, Dr. Pickering had given me instructions to accept *anything*, offered by Dr. Speranski. What had been given to me on October 13, 1973 seemed to be espionage material, putting my life at risk—and my home in Pasadena was far away.

Memories returned of being eight years old (about 1949) and living with my grandparents. We watched the P-51D Mustang fighter airplanes, with their black and white Normandy Invasion stripes arriving at the Van Nuys, California, Air National Guard Base. I said to my grandfather, "I wish I was big so I could fight in the war." He got down to my eye level and said, "There is a war for every generation, you haven't missed anything." The reason I was with my grandparents was because my asthmatic attacks disappeared when I was in Van Nuys rather than at home in Los Angeles. My mom and dad, decided the difference was the better air in rural Van Nuys rather than in LA. When I became older, I discovered I am very allergic to tobacco smoke, solving the mystery as my parents were heavy smokers and my grandparents, non-smokers.

I recalled my final physical examination when I was in the process of resigning my National Oceanic and Atmospheric Administration (NOAA), Officer Corps commission in late 1968. The medical officer had me exhale as hard as I could while he listened to my lungs. He immediately asked if I had ever had asthma, and I answered yes, as a young child. He said, "With asthmatic symptoms like these, you should have been classified as 4F and never been in uniformed service and certainly not as a commissioned officer." I replied, "Well that is interesting, but it doesn't matter now."

A strange chain of events occurred to me. I reasoned that I needed the asthma in order to have extended time with my grandfather who said I must be the first one in our family to attend college and further that I should study science and engineering...his words led me to become a commissioned officer involved in a special mission developing a new method of synchronizing clocks on different continents, that—in turn—got me to NASA/Caltech/JPL and the opportunity to form a team working on combining interplanetary navigation and radio astronomy in the pursuit of technology for earthquake prediction, and that got me the invitation to be with Dr. Pickering to the USSR, all of which got me into a situation being an espionage courier with my life in danger. And it all started because I had been a sickly asthmatic kid.

The US/USSR Situation

Information Known to the Dissidents but Not to Me

[In October 1973, the US and the USSR were marshaling military forces on a global scale with special deployments into areas around the Middle East. The US/USSR super powers were resupplying their allies, the US was replenishing conventional weapons to Israel by means of a massive airlift. The Soviet sea-based shipments were moving war materiel to Egypt and Syria. The US was concerned that the Soviet air power might attack our air freighters. To counter the Soviet air threat, the US Navy Sixth Fleet had deployed three aircraft carrier task groups into the Mediterranean Sea. US forces soon totaled 60 nuclear weapons equipped surface vessels and submarines. The Soviets responded with 96 surface and submarine vessels, with nuclear weapons. This situation then became a super power confrontation of 156 warships—a scale much larger than the Cuban Missile Crisis of eleven years earlier.]

Six Months Earlier
The Challenge of the Russian Language

Michael—4, me—32, and Bong—7
September 1973, Pasadena, CA

About six months before my departure, I decided I would make an effort to learn at least some basic Russian to avoid being the "Ugly American," a syndrome where a US traveler in a foreign country makes no effort to speak the local language and insists that English must be spoken for his or her convenience.

The Russian language is challenging because it is based upon a set of symbols dating back to the 9th century in Slavic cultural regions. Czar Peter the Great demanded a unified and standardized written and spoken Russian language based upon the Cyrillic alphabet devised by Saint Cyril with symbols borrowed from Latin and Greek with some invented symbols to make sounds particular to Russian speakers.

A Russian class seemed like a good idea, but my life was already filled with responsibilities: the technology management of JPL Project ARIES (Astronomical Radio Interferometric Earth Surveying) and having a home life with a wife and two children. I decided on an approach that combined Russian language study as a family activity. This notion caught on surprisingly well with the children, ages four and seven, but not at all with my wife. Our adopted children accepted learning a new alphabet, counting, and simple greetings, and that it could be just as much fun as being read typical children's stories at bedtime. Seven-year-old daughter Bong (a war-injured child from Viet Nam, whose name means flower, and who was receiving frequent surgeries for bullet and shrapnel injuries) managed to memorize the entire 33 character Cyrillic alphabet and some phrases. Michael, age four, an American Indian boy, learned some of the alphabet, some counting, and seemed to like marching around the backyard repeating *"Zdrah-stu-it-eh,"* a hello greeting. I was pleased to discover that my children didn't actually care about their usual children's stories. They enjoyed the time I was spending with them—a wonderful life lesson for me.

In the meantime, by late September 1973, I had made

significant progress so that I could be at least polite and able to travel. I also managed to translate the technical abstract of my presentation into Russian and practiced reading the one page abstract as part of my coming formal presentation in the USSR.

In the process of developing these language skills, I was cautioned that—as in all countries— there are regional accents, and I should probably choose to emulate the manner of speaking used by the people with the most influence. So, I decided I would pay special attention to the men from Moscow to learn the manner and tempo of their speaking.

Once I became immersed in a Russian language environment on a daily basis, my speaking skill improved substantially. That created an unanticipated negative. Apparently, I could speak whole phrases without an accent. More specifically, I was once told (when in the USSR) I sounded like someone from Moscow, which I initially took as a compliment, but then I noticed a couple of people at the table who seemed uneasy. I began to realize I might have created suspicion that I was actually a KGB plant to discover disloyal Soviet citizens who were attempting to establish contacts outside the USSR, which was against Soviet law. I then decided not to be such a proper language student.

Black Sea to the USSR

Life-preserver, in Russian,
top-*ARMENIA*, bottom-ODESSA

While still in Pasadena, I talked with Dick Davies about how he planned to travel to Baku. I decided to follow his advice that we needed time to accommodate the coming eleven hours of jetlag and spend a while getting time zone acclimated. Davies and his wife, Gwendolyn, planned to fly to Istanbul and then cruise on the Black Sea aboard a Soviet ship, entering the USSR at Odessa in the Ukraine. The notion of a Soviet *cruise* ship seemed an oxymoron to me, but I was willing to give it a try.

I arrived in Istanbul aboard a British Airway flight from London in the afternoon of October 2nd. A cab ride got me to the harbor, and I located my ship; however, boarding did not begin until after 6 pm. I carried my briefcase as I walked, but my suitcase had been directly transferred from the airplane to the cruise ship.

At this time, a quite unexpected encounter occurred. A well-dressed man, perhaps 50 years old, stopped to talk with me. He was accompanied by two quite attractive young women, both about 20 years old, one on each arm. The conversation began with questions trying to establish a language we had in common. The man started with what I thought was Turkic, then Italian, and I responded with English, then German, and then Russian. We apparently had no language in common. He said "French Letter" accompanied by head gestures to the women and then displayed a lot of paper money: British, Italian, and French currencies. Although not a common American English term, I assumed the man was trying to purchase condoms which he might think I had with me. I pretended not to understand what he was requesting and kept saying I was sorry but I could not help him. My immediate concern was why this man was soliciting an item which in Western countries was easily available—but apparently was not in Istanbul, Turkey, an Islamic country. This situation seemed likely to turn into a serious problem, so I decided it was best to continue to play dumb, wave farewell, and simply walk away. This trio continued to follow me at a distance for another hour or more. The time was approaching when I would be allowed to board the cruise ship, so I headed to the boarding gate. The trio then approached me again and the man tried once more to purchase "French Letters," now right outside the entry to the passenger boarding area. I thought this quite strange. I briefly considered the possibility that these three persons were actually a surveillance team, but why me?

I entered the boarding zone, presented my US Passport to the Turkish port security police, and was immediately detained. The police began questioning me in a foreign language, presumably Turkic. The loud and animated questioning seemed to involve their belief that I had presented a false passport. A man dressed in a business suit was also in the boarding area and, from that distance, observed the security police questioning me. After a few minutes, this man stepped forward and presented credentials to the port police, retrieved my passport, and took me aside to introduce himself as being from the US Embassy at Istanbul. The embassy official then gave me a rapid quiz session. What is your business? Why are you here? Where did you go to school? Explain the structure of the American political system? Who are your elected members of Congress? What sports teams are in your hometown? I easily passed the questioning and the US Embassy Officer handed back my passport and yelled something in Turkic at the port police who appeared chastised, and I proceeded to board the Soviet *Motor Ship Armenia*. I was fortunate that a US

Embassy person had been available exactly when needed. Later, I suspected it was not a coincidence.

It was near local midnight when the *Armenia* began its process of getting underway by releasing the heavy lines that held this approximately 250-foot ship securely to the dock. Five years earlier, I had been in uniform as electronics officer aboard the *Discoverer*, a state-of-the-art oceanographic vessel, where I had collateral duties to stand bridge watches and be involved in the safe operation of the vessel. As such, I knew the typical procedures of ship operations and the international rules of the nautical road. Although seriously jet-lagged and groggy, I was aware that the Soviet captain of the *M/S Armenia* was "playing chicken" in the Istanbul harbor zone by sounding eminent at-sea collision warnings, five or more rapid blasts of the horn. These rapid horn blasts caused me to search for a life jacket within my individual passenger cabin, where I found no safety equipment of any sort— rather unsettling. At the same time, no announcements were being made aboard the ship in any language. This bullying behavior seemed to be standard operating procedure, and fortunately, there was no at-sea collision but merely a tactic to clear the way for his vessel to proceed, regardless of who had the right-of-way by international law.

After a few hours of not so restful sleep, I awoke to the appearance of daylight out of my cabin porthole and the feeling of seasickness, realizing it had been about five years since I was last at sea. I decided that it was important for me to eat breakfast in order to get into this time zone, now ten hours ahead of Pasadena. I managed to find my way to the food service area one deck above my cabin. This was the first time I had seen any young Soviets. I had been told it was a highly sought opportunity for a young person to work outside the Soviet Union itself, especially to be aboard a Soviet cruise ship in a warmer climate region such as the Black Sea where a young person could visit other places, such as the bright lights of Varna Bulgaria.

Once in the food service area, I realized that my feelings of nausea were not being helped by the available food: eggs in their shells—maybe hard boiled or raw or way over-cooked and hard cold black bread. Luckily, the tea and sugar were fine. I decided to distract myself by girl-watching. I soon noticed that all these young women were in nylons, but hadn't shaved their legs. This observation caused me to recognize that viewing long strands of dark leg hair escaping from nylon clad legs was not actually helping my seasickness. I decided to make a quick exit from breakfast service. Culture Shock!

Soviet Style Spy Movie

Dr. Richard Davies and his wife, Gwendolyn
aboard *M/S Armenia*, Oct. 1973

Fortunately, the evening meal (wine, desserts, and service) was quite good on the *Armenia*. As the dishes were being cleared, I was surprised to see crew members rolling in a film projector and lowering a movie screen. The after dinner feature was a Soviet spy movie which I expected to be a Soviet version of a James Bond movie. However, this film began with a stern lecture delivered by an elderly high ranking and uniformed Soviet Air Force officer, lecturing about the threat to the USSR way of life posed by hostile western nations. The film was, of course, mostly in Russian dialogue except for some poorly spoken English by actors playing British and Americans. These "bad guy" performances bordered at times on the rather comical. The story line depicted a dedicated group of essentially faceless Soviet security committee members who apprehend the American and British operatives attempting to steal air defense secrets.

The following morning, I met Gwendolyn Davies on the uppermost deck as we looked through the haze at Varna Bulgaria where the *M/S Armenia* would not be making a scheduled port call because of a local cholera outbreak–so much for the "bright-lights." Gwendolyn was well-versed in the arts and a film connoisseur. She asked if I had noticed the firm hand of the Soviet Communist Party in the film plot. I said I supposed I had, but I invited her analysis. She pointed out that "the plot emphasized the intrinsic strength of State-conducted collective action and not individualism." She further conjectured that the film was in stark contrast to the heroic individuals of the western tradition, e.g., James Bond, who assesses situations and takes individual initiative, usually against explicit command directives, and solves major problems. I agreed with her analysis.

Entering the USSR at Odessa, Ukraine Republic

Potemkin Steps in Odessa, Ukraine with the *M/S Armenia* at dock, October 1973

These steps are a piece of cinematic history deriving from a 1925 film by Sergei Eisenstein, *Battleship Potemkin*, depicting the 1905 failed mutiny against the Tsarist regime. This film included a scene of a lone baby carriage cascading down the staircase.

Upon *M/S Armenia's* arrival at Odessa in the Soviet Republic of Ukraine, all passengers were escorted to the Soviet port security police area. The police conducted a detailed search of my luggage and briefcase that included a careful inspection of the mechanical structure of each case accomplished by the security officer running his hands over the seams, brackets, and latches— searching for hidden compartments, I supposed. This included the contents of every pocket in my clothing and every item of money in any form. My camera, photos, all printed material, and my technical paper for presentation in Baku received attention. They were especially interested in the book I was reading, *Jonathan Livingston Seagull.*

"What is this book about?" the port security officer barked.

"It is a book about birds," I answered, without any mention of nonconforming behavior.

Baku, USSR, 8 October 1973

V. I. Lenin, International Conference Center,
Venue of the International Astronautical Congress,
BAKU, USSR

On my first day in Baku, an official cocktail party reception for all of the conference participants had been planned for the early evening. Being eleven time zones jetlagged, I nearly slept through the party time. Stumbling into the large venue, which was absolutely jammed, I couldn't figure out where the food and drinks were being provided.

At that point, three women came up to me, already knowing my name and from whence in the US I haled. They asked me why I did not have a glass of champagne or any hors d'oeuvres. I replied that I had no idea where to find such food and drink.

"Wait right here," one instructed, and all three disappeared to re-emerge in a couple of minutes with the provender. However, there was no place for me to sit or a table for the provisions.

"This is no problem," one said, and then all three stood holding my loaded plate and glass while I consumed the refreshments. This reminded me of my JPL security briefing, warning how Americans were compromised in the Soviet Union by women, although at this point, the attention seemed helpful.

These women, my food service squad, said they were from a research institute and that they were mathematicians.

"What kind of research?"

Answer: commodities production and distribution done manually rather than the common approach at that time in the US which utilized large scale computing machines. Their research did not involve any contact with the world in which I performed *my* research, defined by the laws of physics. I also recalled from my security briefing that the sort of women who compromised Americans were much more than just average attractive women, but also had beautiful smiles probably rendered by dentists in Norway. In the case of these three women, they were not particularly good looking nor did they appear to be the beneficiaries of extensive dental work.

In our conversation, I repeated what I had heard about the

main principle guiding the economic structure of the Soviet Union: "from each according to ability, to each according to need." The three women then began to recite Russian phrases probably learned as young students. They laughed as if the remembered phrases were rather silly.

"I have two small children at home and, even on a small family scale," I admitted, "it's difficult, to put that ability/need concept into practice. I can't understand how it works in a society with hundreds of millions of people." I smiled in commiseration.

The women only smiled to one another in response.

We Must Run—Now

Wednesday October 10th, after the morning technical sessions— perhaps ten sessions ran concurrently—the three women appeared outside the specific meeting room where I was and invited me to lunch.

The restaurant was some distance away from the V.I. Lenin Palace conference venue, and it was necessary to ride on the subway. (In retrospect, I can see that these young women were engaged in more than a simple "get acquainted" opportunity. Instead, they were probably involved in a vetting process which likely had begun as soon as I arrived at the conference as they had been present at my conference registration and check-in processing though I had been too jet-lagged and sleepy to remember at that time. Other Soviet scientists and engineers about my age were part of these overtly social meetings at meals and during informal walking chats. *Is all this socializing related to whether I can be trusted?* I wondered.

The subway entrance was not obvious and seemed to have no signs, but the women were locals and moved with obvious familiarity. The initial entry was by means of a steep, rapidly descending escalator that arrived at a large central landing. High overhead was a sizable dome with intricately inlayed ceramic tile patterns. I took out my small pocket camera, pointed it up at the dome, and pressed the shutter release. The camera was a recent purchase for this trip, and I had forgotten that the internal electronics would determine when the light level needed to have a flash lamp assist. The camera flash occurred at about the same instant that one of the women said that it was not allowed to take photographs inside the subway. One of the other women said that a young teenage boy had seen me take the photo and was running away and one of the women said, "That boy is looking for a 'milliman'"—Soviet Army personnel assigned to law enforcement within cities. In a deadly serious voice, Nadia said to me, "We must run now." Then all three women moved quickly, scanning the area and being careful that I was not lost in the crowd. The four of us ran down the steep and fast moving escalators that descended to a depth of perhaps another one or two hundred feet to a network of subway platforms. Then we moved in and out of multiple trains, boarding a final car as the doors were closing. This train riding and car switching continued two more times at other stations and finally ended up near the restaurant—our original destination before the evasive maneuvers had begun. I promised not to take any more photos of the subway which Nadia said would be a good idea.

Once at the restaurant, another young Soviet scientist, Vasiliy (not his actual name) from Moscow, joined us. The group began to discuss what it was like growing up in our different societies in the post-World War II era. Vasiliy couldn't believe my stories of "drop drills" in schools where students were trained to get under school desks, placing hands over the tops of our heads as we faced away from the windows. These drills were motivated by the belief that Soviet bombers were being prepared to drop atomic bombs on American cities. I asked if the USSR student believed that the US was planning to bomb the USSR and what were the people of the cities supposed to do to protect themselves. Vasiliy did not seem to want to discuss such a topic but decided to reply with a sort of a joke.

"If American bombers are coming, people are to pull white sheets over their heads and slowly crawl to the nearest cemetery. It is important to crawl slowly because running might create a panic." I regarded this "joke" as a sort of grim insight into the Soviet worldview, one that didn't seem to have an American parallel.

I asked about the Soviet educational policy, a practice I had heard occurred early in a student's life, where decisions were made about each person's occupation in adult life, such as scientist, teacher, musician, soldier, manual worker, etc. I opined that such polices seemed quite unfair, but my Soviet friends shrugged their shoulders and Vasiliy said that it was "just the way it is."

Questions were casually asked regarding what I knew about the history of the Soviet "Great Patriotic War" (World War II) and what had happened in the USSR during those years. These Soviets were concerned that Americans had a cavalier attitude about war because neither of the world wars had happened in the American continental homeland. They feared that the American public's ignorance of war's human consequences might make conflict between the US and the USSR somehow acceptable. My new Soviet acquaintances wanted to know about my home life. I told them I was married and had two children, an adopted American Indian boy, four years old and a war-injured orphan Vietnamese girl, who had just turned eight years old. I shared photos of my family.

"Is it common for American families to take in war-injured children?" I was asked, and I replied that it did not happen often. My new friends did not carry photos of their families, which I thought was curious, but I did not pursue the topic further. We exchanged brief stories about remembering the war years and their family's involvements in WW II, although all of us had been rather young in those years. My Soviet friends reminded me that in the

USSR, the toll in those war years had been 26 million deaths, only nine million of which had been combatants. We all agreed that the US and the USSR must never go to war.

Evening of 12 October
Pickering's Room Search

Following the conclusion of the formal dinner for all the senior members of the conference delegations, Dr. Speranski learned from the Baku Hotel staff that KGB had entered Pickering's room during dinnertime. Speranski concluded that Pickering was under suspicion and would be ordered out of the USSR. Looking back, it seems obvious to me that this was seen as the time to engage the main plan, the original strategy created months earlier: I, MacDoran, had to become the courier of the *bona fides* documents required to establish the back channel to the US Government. Time was of the essence, especially because of the rapidly deteriorating situation of the Yom Kippur War. Dr. Speranski knew that JPL Director Pickering and his associates had high level US Government access. Such high level connections were vital to defusing the looming threat of global war most likely to cascade into a nuclear catastrophe. Pickering was well known within the US Congressional Committees, especially Defense and Science, and known more widely to the American public, having twice been on the cover of *Time Magazine*. Also, Pickering's deputy—Charles H. Terhune, a retired US Air Force Lieutenant General (three stars)—had personal friendships at senior levels of the Department of Defense and the Central Intelligence Agency (CIA).

Events Known to the Dissidents, But Not to Me

The White House

[During October 1973, the Nixon White House was significantly distracted by the crumbling cover-up of the Watergate Affair and further complicated by President Nixon's persistent consumption of alcohol, which caused Dr. Henry Kissinger to refer to Nixon as "our drunk friend." Adding to the dysfunction was the resignation of Vice President Spiro Agnew who was under threat of indictment for bribery. In the absence of a vice president, the order of succession would pass the presidency to the Speaker of the House, Carl Albert, a Democrat. The White House viewed such an event as being counter to the results of the 1972 election. There was also the so-called "Saturday Night Massacre" in which Nixon fired officials within his administration who refused to fire the Watergate Special Prosecutor, Archibald Cox.

The net effect was a vacuum of elected leadership within the Executive Branch. It is within this environment that Kissinger, in a dual capacity as Secretary of State and National Security Advisor together with US Army General Alexander Haig, as the White House Chief of Staff, maneuvered themselves into the roles of the principal foreign policy makers for the United States Government. An additional alarming likelihood was that General Haig was attempting to gain possession of the "football," the DoD briefcase-like device that issues cryptographic text which enables the President (or whomever possesses the device) to authorize launching US nuclear armed intercontinental ballistic missiles (ICBM) at targets in the Soviet Union.

Henry Kissinger relied on a CIA operative, Edwin

P. Wilson, who was able to accomplish what Kissinger needed done. Kissinger focused on results and preferred to be uncurious about the details of how Wilson got things done. An example: Kissinger wanted to replace William P. Rogers as Secretary of State. Wilson managed staffing changes that effectively installed political spies into State Department offices. Those spies harvested drafts of working papers that allowed Kissinger to undermine Rogers' effectiveness which was noticed by President Nixon and resulted in Rogers' resignation. President Nixon then selected Kissinger to become the new Secretary of State and allowed him to retain his prior position as National Security Advisor.

While at the CIA, E. P. Wilson was under investigation for having made tens of millions of dollars from his own "businesses" under the guise of official CIA missions, involving illegal transactions (such as selling restricted American weapons —C4 plastic explosives with detonation timers, spy ships, state-of-art NSA secure communications equipment) and drug trafficking out of Southeast Asia. E. P. Wilson even had his own international bank, Nugan Hand Bank, operations to launder money. In October 1973, Wilson was a contract employee to the Office of Naval Intelligence (ONI) and assigned to Task Force-157, operating near Istanbul, Turkey. TF-157 monitored Soviet shipments of military supplies moving on the Black Sea, through the Bosporus Strait, and into the Mediterranean Sea heading to Egypt and Syria. As had been the earlier situation at the CIA, the ONI started its own investigation of Wilson's personal business dealings and was preparing to cancel his ONI contract. Wilson devised a plan whereby he would appear indispensable to the highest level US Government person known to him, Dr. Henry Kissinger. Wilson had retained possession of some of the NSA secure ROGER channel communications equipment from his earlier involvement in the 1971 Nixon opening to the People's Republic of China, (PRC). Kissinger required the secure communications capability in order to prevent the DoD, CIA, or the State Department from knowing about his negotiations with the Chinese. On 24 October, Wilson sent a TF-157 FLASH, highest urgency message, from Istanbul to Kissinger at the White House, reporting the detection of Soviet nuclear weapons in transit to Egypt in the midst of the Yom Kippur War. This report of a nuclear weapons shipment to Egypt contributed to the elevation of US military readiness to DEFCON 3 which placed US Armed Forces on a global alert against possible Soviet threats to US interests. (DEFCON 1 is a global war status for all US Armed Forces.)]

The ROGER Channel

[The KGB had gained access to the ROGER channel encrypted communication equipment, possibly from one of Wilson's previous illegal sales of such NSA equipment to Libya, although similar cryptographic equipment had been captured from an Israeli listening post by Syrian military units on the first day of the Yom Kippur War. Libya had close contact with the Soviets and such equipment would have been quickly bartered and transferred to the KGB. It was KGB possession of this equipment that allowed the USSR to read the highest levels of US Government communications. The KGB thus had the means to know of the false Wilson report to Kissinger of a Soviet nuclear weapons shipment to Egypt. Dissidents within the Kremlin soon learned of the Wilson report …and knew it was false. In late October, the Soviet dissidents needed the back channel to the US Government more than ever. The dissidents likely believed that the report of nuclear weapons under Egyptian control could cause Israel to execute a preemptive nuclear weapons first strike —likely starting a global nuclear war. Henry Kissinger characterized the Yom Kippur War events as leading to the "annihilation of humanity."]

A Tourist in Moscow —15 October

At the beginning of my post-conference tour, the first scenic trip was to Moscow and a bus ride around the city. The Moscow streets were quite wide, perhaps three times the width common in large American cities. I presumed that street widths were required for the rapid deployment of military equipment and logistical support of war fighting equipment. The tour bus passed within about a quarter mile of some massive buildings, perhaps forty stories high, from which were hung an enormous banner with large faces.

There were a few Americans on this tour bus, and someone asked, "Who are the people on the banner?" Before our tour guide could answer, I volunteered that the three men were "Manny, Mo, and Jack" (the PEP Boys, of auto parts fame in the US).

"You are incorrect," the tour guide said. "The three men are Marx, Engels, and Lenin."

The Americans onboard the tour bus understood the joke, a reference to a bit of American car culture. Some humor helped lighten my tension, and, I supposed, made me feel less a spy, more like a tourist having fun.

We passed by a section of foreign embassies which included the US Embassy. I paid close attention to this part of the tour. Soviet military police were clearly visible. So, exiting the bus with the documents that had been entrusted to me, perhaps under my clothing, might be possible. On the other hand, Soviet security personnel in the vicinity of the US Embassy made getting even to the gate unlikely. An additional complication was that Soviet hotels always collected the passports of "guests," retrievable only by the Intourist Guides who controlled where their tourists went. Lacking my US passport greatly complicated my ability to identify myself quickly as a US citizen, in which case, I feared, I would shortly be in the hands of Soviet security personnel and then the KGB.

The following morning, I faked being sick in order not to go on the scheduled morning tour in Moscow. Curious about whether I was being followed, I walked around the city dressed in a nondescript black winter coat, using a cartoonish version of a city map, and with sufficient Russian language skills to move about on the subway. I found that I apparently blended in because as I studied the overhead display boards of the subway trains, Soviet locals actually asked me for directions.

"I am sorry," I said, using a short response in Russian I had composed, "but I am a visitor and speak only a little Russian." People just grunted and hurried off to find the right subway train. The only spy craft I knew came from having read an early Ian Fleming, James Bond book, when I was in grad school and sick with the flu. The story described how Mr. Bond stood looking in a shop window while actually focusing on the glass —a "first-surface" reflection of the scene behind him. In the cold Moscow autumn, with a lot of people in drab dark clothing, it was difficult to tell if the same people were reappearing in the rearview scene, even with a tactic of doubling back and then checking for familiar faces behind me.

The temptation to have my briefcase (with the *bona fides* documents) with me all the time was strong, but I was supposed to be a tourist at this stage of my trip. Carrying my briefcase, I felt, would only serve to invite questions as to why I needed to have it all the time. So, though it bothered me, the briefcase needed to remain in my hotel room unless I was in travel status or when I had been at the space conference.

Then there was the matter of whether or not my hotel room was under surveillance and being searched. A version of a James Bond's method: Careful alignment of an unlocked or even open briefcase relative to wall corners or window frames could be assessed visually. Or carefully set alignments of file folders would detect even slight movement caused by a search. In these ways, I concluded that my briefcase was not being searched when I was away from my hotel room.

Students at a Science Museum

While walking the Moscow city streets, I came upon a local school science museum and decided to go in. At a large exhibit booth, a man was explaining Soviet communications satellites to a group of about fifty high school age students, both boys and girls. About a dozen students at the front were paying close attention to every word, while a middle section of students sort of dozed off while managing to remain standing, and at the back of the group, about two dozen students participated in a game, known in the American vernacular, as "grab-ass." Three teachers were trying to maintain some semblance of order but were clearly losing the battle. When the time arrived to get back on the bus, a student was apparently missing. A teacher roamed the halls calling "Mischa." I watched this slice of teenage Soviet real-life and felt a confusing double wave of hopefulness and dread. American and Soviet societies are rather similar, and there is real hope for all of us—*but only if the BIG people don't destroy everything.*

Part 3

Possible Vladimir Putin Involvement

[The ongoing Yom Kippur War likely put a strain on KGB Counter Intelligence resources, and personnel in training had been put into the field with their trainers. One such individual would have been 21-year-old Vladimir Vladimirovich Putin who was in training at Leningrad to become an intelligence officer as his father before him had been in the NKVD (predecessor of the KGB). As we all know, this individual rose in prominence in Russia. Putin was being trained in the German language for later deployment to West Germany. In the Dick Davies situation following the IAF conference, a young man, about 20 years old, had surveilled Davies and his wife after the conference and engaged Davies in long conversations about physics—possibly as the Davies' luggage was being searched. The young man was later concluded to be KGB, probably in training and likely with a training officer in the vicinity.]

Leningrad, USSR

Peter MacDoran at the monument

of Peter the Great

in Leningrad, USSR in October 1973

In Leningrad, the Intourist guide was an attractive young woman, Anastasia (not her actual name) who appeared to have had the benefits of orthodontia, making me suspicious because of my pre-trip security briefing. Anastasia learned I was an American space scientist and volunteered that she had been educated as a radio engineer. I asked why she wasn't doing engineering, and she replied that her physician mother had arranged for her to spend some time as an Intourist Guide to improve English language skills. As the bus travelled around to the various government approved tourist sites, Anastasia and I talked about our two countries— although, earlier I had told myself not to get into political debates.

"There ain't no such thing as a free lunch," "Right-On," "Cool," "Hip," and "Shacking-up," Anastasia proudly listed her personal collection of American slang expressions.

I asked what she knew about life outside the USSR, since such information was not likely to be available from the leading Soviet newspapers, *Pravda* and *Izvestiya*.

"I listen to Voice of America and the BBC," she replied.

"I learned the Soviet government provided radios at no cost…but those radios were designed to receive only Official Soviet broadcasts…thus only Soviet broadcasts could be received.

"I am a radio engineer so I make changes," Anastasia leveled a glance at me.

This roused my curiosity a great deal as I had been an amateur radio operator since the age of thirteen and had built many receivers over the years.

"What did you actually do that allowed you to listen to such forbidden broadcasts?" I quizzed her. She answered this question credibly. When I asked if such changes were actually allowed, she answered, "Well, I'm still alive." I did not pursue the implications of such an answer.

"I know about the serious problem of drugs in America," Anastasia changed the subject and finished with the shocking statement, "There are no drug problems in the USSR."

"As soon as you can convince me that vodka is not a drug and that alcoholism is not a massive problem in the USSR, then a discussion of US and USSR relative drug problems can be discussed," I quipped. My debates with Anastasia often had a flirtatious tone, and I very much enjoyed the distraction away from the possibility of being arrested at any time. An older woman from the Netherlands who was in the tour group overheard some of our *repartee.*

"You should get to bed sooner," she said, with a smile. I was a bit taken aback by this proper appearing lady, about my mother's age, recommending an extramarital affair. I assumed that her sanction of such things reflected a European lifestyle, and the suggestion was certainly tempting. Fortunately for me, Anastasia was a serious cigarette smoker and possessed a strong ashtray odor. There was also the complication that Soviet society seemed to exhibit a rigid sense of sexual morality bordering on the puritanical...which I did not wish to challenge especially considering the *bona fides* documents entrusted to me...as well as potential later complications when returning home.

However, I did begin to reevaluate Anastasia's apparent benefits of orthodontia and decided they might have been arranged by her physician mother, rather than through special KGB influence to create a female operative for use against selected US individuals.

Soviet Full Employment

The Soviets were proud of their achievement of having a fully employed population, and I agreed that was a worthy achievement. Nonetheless, in at least one instance, the notion of not-clear-on-the-concept seemed to apply. The Hotel Leningrad appeared to be relatively new and modern with a lobby level that had the appearance of a dozen elevators. My impression: It was the same four modern appearing elevators every day, leading me to wonder whether or not there were actually elevator cars in the other eight elevator slots in the main lobby!

The process of getting to one's room consisted of entering an available elevator car and requesting the desired stop to a man standing next to a familiar appearing panel of many buttons with numbers that indicated floors. Back home, such elevators operated by having hotel guests push their own buttons. The process of speaking the floor number continued every day with the elevator operator pushing the button for the passenger. After all, it was not as if it was necessary to announce something like "fifth floor women's lingerie," for example. One morning, I noticed the elevator attendant had a trainee with him, and it seemed the trainee rode the elevator for the entire day…learning how to push buttons, I guess.

Anastasia explained the salary reward structure where the least desirable jobs were paid the most money. However, the reality of better living in Soviet society was achieved by having access to government controlled goods. Thus, possession of many rubles tended to be of little real value. Anastasia gave the example of her physician mother who had access to a car and driver but was paid only 160 rubles per month, while the elderly woman shoveling snow was paid 200 rubles per month. The great many elderly women workers were likely widows of The Great Patriotic War (World War II) and were referred to collectively as *Babushkas* (the term for grandmother which was also applied to a folded head scarf). The usual approach to filling undesirable jobs was to continue to raise the pay for the job until someone agreed to do it. The irony was, of course, that having lots of rubles did not actually allow a person to purchase what was truly wanted, that required political influence.

Doska Pochka

In Leningrad, I continued to be bothered by the whole situation of being in danger and decided to pretend it just wasn't happening. In my past, I had made sort of jokes of problems as a relief mechanism, as I had done while on the Moscow tour bus by suggesting that the three faces on the gigantic hanging banner were Manny, Moe, and Jack, the Pep Boys.

On the official Intourist bus travels around the City of Leningrad, public displays, known as *Doska Pochka*, acknowledged persons doing their jobs well. These award notices were composed of the individual's photograph, his/her name, and a brief job description. Those displayed were in a cylindrical format on a pole. The persons being honored appeared to cover a broad spectrum of Soviet society, from Communist Party officials to members of the military, medical personnel, and the elderly ladies who shoveled snow.

Ticket to the Kirov Ballet

Although not a true aficionado of dance, I decided to improve myself by going to a performance of the world famous Kirov Ballet. So I ventured to the Leningrad Hotel lobby and the Service Bureau desk. The in-room description of hotel services stated that the Service Bureau would be open from "18 to 21 hours" (6 to 9 pm) and ballet ticket purchases could be made there. I consulted my Russian/English dictionary so I could politely request a ticket.

A little past 6:30 pm, I arrived at the Service Bureau desk and politely stated, in Russian, my wish to purchase a ticket to the Kirov Ballet.

The woman replied in English that the Service Bureau was closed. I responded that the sign on her desk said it was open for business at 6 pm and that it was then 6:40 pm. My reporting to her of the current local time seemed not to have the desired effect.

"You speak English, yes?" She glared at me. "The Service desk is closed."

I retreated back to my hotel room and decided to make a little *Doska Pochka* award for the woman at the bureau desk, whose name I remembered, denoting her particular achievement had been "Rudeness Conducted in The English Language." I planned to stick the award notice on the side of her desk in the lobby, although I actually lacked adhesive tape.

At about the time I had completed this award notice preparation, a knock on my hotel room door announced Antonio (not his actual name), an Italian graduate student who had recently joined our Intourist travel group. He asked what I was working on, and I described my non-ticket acquisition adventure and the *Doska Pochka* notice.

"Are you totally insane?" His fully animated manner was that which only a native Italian can deliver. "These people have no sense of humor, and they are going to arrest you, and they are going to arrest me too because I even know you."

Immediately, I began to consider the merits of Antonio's socio-political assessment, realizing that if I were arrested for anything at all, my briefcase was likely to be searched, and Speranski's *bona fides* documents intended for Pickering would be found…and I would be in the hands of the KGB in short order.

"You are probably correct, Antonio, and I promise to give up that little project." We agreed to meet down at the hotel lobby bar and he left.

I tore my *Doska Pochka* notice into quite small pieces and put them in my pocket to dispose of in a downstairs restroom. This small incident snapped me back into the reality of my situation—that I was at serious personal risk and had to be more careful.

Entering the lobby bar, I encountered the older Dutch couple and asked, "How are you doing?" and related my hotel "service bureau" encounter and the "no Kirov ballet ticket" event.

The woman questioned whether I had been sufficiently polite to the lady at the Service Bureau desk.

"A patient man I, down to my fingertips, the sort who never could, never would, let an insulting remark escape his lips," I quoted from the musical *My Fair Lady*. Fortunately, my Dutch friends were familiar with that particular British stage play. The proper Dutch woman responded with a somewhat quizzical expression, and then gave me a small smile.

Strange "Coincidences"

The following early evening, October 20, I was scheduled to depart the Hotel Leningrad for the airport in order to fly back to Moscow, a required stop in order to proceed onto my flight to Tokyo. I arrived at the lobby with my briefcase, and a hotel porter brought my suitcase to me. While I was saying goodbyes to some of my fellow tour group friends, the husband of the Dutch couple said he would tell the front desk I needed a cab to go to the airport.

The cab arrived and I was the only passenger. My suitcase was loaded into the back seat with me, and I placed my briefcase under my legs to keep it close. The weather was rather cold with light snow and a chilly breeze.

After only a few minutes of the cab ride, the driver inserted a cassette tape into the dashboard player, and the *My Fair Lady* music and lyrics, in English, began to play and precisely at the lyrics, "A patient man am I, down to my fingertips, the sort who never could, never would, let an insulting remark escape his lips." This was an exceptionally odd circumstance, especially since the cab driver seemed to speak no English. I then thought about the astronomically long odds against such music and those lyrics occurring at random in the USSR in a cab with me alone, replaying words I had spoken to the Dutch couple the previous evening. I thought, what is going on?

I decided to settle back and watch the road traffic and the

snow falling. This triggered recollections of other odd coincidences on this trip: For example, my 2 October detention by the Istanbul, Turkey port security police as I entered the ship boarding area where the US Embassy official just happened to be available to solve the issue of whether the port police would halt my boarding the *M/S Armenia* and how I had been followed by the well-dressed man, with the two young female companions, who wanted me to sell him "French Letters." That trio had caused me to be under surveillance for a couple of hours and had followed me to the ship boarding gate and must have been seen by the US Embassy officer.

At the time, I considered it a fortunate event that a US Embassy person had been available exactly when needed. However, now—riding in a Leningrad cab—I began to consider the probability of a pair or maybe even three long-shot coincidences, first in Istanbul and now in Leningrad. Maybe these events were intended to communicate that I had unknown friends who were looking out for me. But I had no way of knowing who or where they were.

Moscow and the Snowstorm

After departing Leningrad, I was required to return to Moscow in order to proceed to Tokyo; however, a severe snowstorm was closing down travel from the Moscow region. I was originally scheduled for one night at the largest hotel in the world, the Rossiya, with 3,200 rooms. But the storm had caused frozen pipes, rendering half the rooms of this mammoth accommodation unusable.

This seemed curious. Certainly cold weather issues such as frozen water pipes must be a routinely managed challenge in that part of the world. How could such a major event have happened making 1,600 rooms unusable, with the associated challenge of disrupted reservations…and just because of the snow? Of course, I reasoned with myself, the storm was substantial enough to shut down the airport—no flights in or out.

Confusion began as it became necessary for travelers to double up into remaining functional hotel rooms. At that point, my name mysteriously disappeared from the list of persons to be reassigned to another hotel. Earlier, I had seen my name in English letters typed on a sheet and had memorized the Russian names before and after mine.

Suddenly, where my name had been were Cyrillic letters!

Perhaps those were a transliteration of MacDoran…except that these Cyrillic letter sounds did **not** reproduce the sound of my name—"MacDoran."

Using both Russian and English, I tried to alert the lady who was managing the hotel reassignments. She acted as if she had not heard or understood what I was saying in either language. Odd, as I was sure I had heard her speaking English a couple of hours earlier.

Fear gripped me as I began to feel I was about to be made to disappear. Looking back, I wonder if that was exactly the intent.

After a few uneasy hours of waiting, I was informed that my hotel assignment had been shifted to an older but quite elegant hotel, the Metropol. Upon my mid-evening arrival there, the usual check-in procedure was followed—my passport was taken and the porter was given my room key.

Arriving at my assigned room, I was glad to see my suitcase had already arrived. I had also hoped to meet the man with whom I was to share this room—another American, I'd been told. There was evidence that I had a roommate who was not there.

I decided to leave my briefcase in the room (as I've said before—too suspicious looking to bring it) and ventured out to find some food, maybe a beer, though Soviet beer left a lot to be desired. The hotel elevator had notices of meeting locations. One, in German, was for a DDR (German Democratic Republic, AKA East Germany) Communist Party Youth Congress and one was an advertisement for a bar at the hotel roof level. I headed for the bar.

Judging from the manner of dress and many languages being spoken, here seemed to be persons from all over the world. At the bar, I noticed some people with what appeared to be orange juice drinks, so when the bartender asked (in English) what I wanted, I replied a "screwdriver" and a ham sandwich.

"Are you an American?" he asked, and I nodded yes.

"The oranges came today—from Israel. The Jews grow wonderful oranges," he shared. A radio on a shelf behind the bar was playing American style music from about the 1940s era.

As I waited for my drink and food, the music abruptly stopped and an English language newscaster read a statement: The United States had just declared a Defense Condition 3 effective immediately as of midnight the 24th of October, Washington time. US Armed Forces were now on a worldwide alert for hostile actions by the Soviet military. The announcer's text was repeated, but now with a comment that the term "Defense Condition" was commonly referred to as DEFCON and that this radio station would relay any further developments. The broadcast music suddenly returned, and for several seconds, not a word was said in the bar. Then, it seemed everyone was talking at once. I sat on my barstool watching the commotion.

"What does DEFCON 3 mean?" the bartender asked me.

"I don't know…but it doesn't sound like anything good."

I decided to head back to my room perhaps to meet my roommate. Across from the elevator, the windows of this roof level venue displayed a lovely view of the Kremlin across the river, the surrounding city below with its thousands of shimmering lights and wind driven snowflakes fluttering by.

At that moment, I imagined waving my arms at the US Air Force officers in the missile silos in the middle of some farm fields in the American Midwest, their hands hovering above fire-condition launch switches of inter-continental ballistic missiles.

"Hey, guys, don't shoot," I visualized myself yelling.

My grim imaginings were suddenly interrupted by four college-age German Communist Party students, one guy and three young women. They were quite drunk and apparently unaware of the announcement of the US global declaration of DEFCON 3. For a brief instant, I considered speaking some German to them. I had studied it in order to pass my foreign language requirement while in grad school, but I reconsidered the idea as being incompatible with trying to remain unnoticed, especially considering the probable search of my briefcase tomorrow which could lead to my arrest. Given the highly inebriated condition of the three women and one guy, the possible recruitment of one more guy for the party was a complication I didn't need. I stood quietly in the elevator as we descended a few floors where I got off and the noisy foursome continued blissfully on their way, completely unaware that the gears of potential global destruction were engaging.

The youthful students' innocence in stark contrast with the gravity of DEFCON 3 reminded me of a time in 1964 when I was a graduate student at the University of California, Santa Barbara. My physics professors, 20 years earlier, had been J. Robert Oppenheimer's students involved in the World War II, Manhattan Project. They told of the reaction of Professor Oppenheimer after the project team witnessed the detonation of the first nuclear weapon. He was initially silent and then quoted Vishnu from the *Hindu Bhagavad Gita*, "I am Become Death, the Destroyer of Worlds."

DEFCON 3

[The USAF, Strategic Air Command, began the redeployment of more than fifty nuclear armed B-52D inter-continental strategic bombers from the Guam US Air Force Base to US continental air bases as a contingency against the USSR if the DEFCON status was once more elevated.
Israel responded to the US DEFCON 3 status by arming its nuclear weapons, for a second time, during the Yom Kippur War, on 25 October.
Note: The National Security Archive has no record of President Nixon having signed the 1973 DEFCON 3 order.]

Avoiding a Search

I returned to my assigned hotel room and met the man who purported to be an "American diplomat," although I had no way of knowing who he actually was.

He said his name was James (not the name that had been told to me), and he said he was on the faculty of an Ivy League university. James said he had been involved in a bilateral US/USSR working group, and diplomatic friction had developed that required more late night meetings. James indicated that the meeting from which he had just returned involved a higher-level Soviet official who issued directives to the other Soviet working group members that James was to be shown much better levels of cooperation.

James said I had already met one of the committee members, the husband of the Dutch couple in my Leningrad tour group. That man was also a member of the Club of Rome, an international group of diplomats and academics specializing in negotiating in the world's hotspots. The next Club of Rome meeting was being held in Tokyo, and it was hoped a cease-fire to the Yom Kippur War could be achieved.

The snowstorm continued for another full day, and I spent several hours and mealtimes with about a dozen diplomats— mainly from European and Soviet-Bloc countries. I heard over and over again about the complexities of United Nations Resolutions 242 and 338 and whether the French word for "territory" (always used in UN Resolutions) was a singular or plural word…and human lives were being lost over such a nuance.

The Dutch diplomat, a former general in the Royal Dutch Air Force had recently returned to the Metropol Hotel after his visit to the Dutch embassy in Moscow. He began a briefing to his colleagues and to me with some of the history of the special relationship between Israel and the Dutch dating back to the late 1930s and into World War II. The Dutch had provided safe harbor for many Jews (e.g., *The Diary of Anne Frank*) as the Nazis were conducting mass arrests and transporting thousands of Jews to concentration camps and subsequently murdering millions of them.

The Israelis discussed what was happening in the Middle East. The evening before the 6 October attacks on Israel by Egypt and Syria, a briefing had been given by the Israel Defense Forces, General Moshe Dayan to President Golda Meir. Dayan had stated that Arab attacks would begin in a few hours. President Meir said an attack actually had to happen because US assistance was likely to be needed. Israel had been warned not to initiate another preemptive attack as had occurred in 1967 when Israel had essentially destroyed the Egyptian Air Force within a few hours. The US warning came with an advisory that a repeat of preemptive attacks would result in delayed assistance from the US.

"We must allow Israel to be clearly attacked, and I know it will cost me my reelection," Israeli President Meir had said.

When it came time to depart Moscow on October 25th, the diplomatic group members numbered about twenty, and they were gathered in their own group. I got into a line that had an X-ray machine imaging carry-on items, especially looking for weapons. On the other side of that machine, airport security officers were setting up what appeared to be a detailed inspection of things being carried by passengers.

At this point, I became more than a little apprehensive, remembering the kind of search I had experienced on my arrival at the Black Sea Port of Odessa when entering the Soviet Union about three weeks earlier.

I rehearsed a kind of story that the envelope contained a summary of Soviet space achievements and were available at several places around the exhibit hall in Baku. I had simply picked one of them up.

If challenged, I would say I hadn't paid much attention to what was in the envelope. I'd act surprised, "Why? What is in it?" It sounded plausible to me, but if I was actually grilled over the contents, I wasn't so confident how well I would hold up. After all, I wasn't trained for this kind of stuff.

To get calmer, I forced myself to think about the

photographs I had made with my small camera using 110 film cartridges. Before the trip, I had purchased a lead-lined carrying bag especially designed for film going through airport X-ray machines. The bag contained both fresh and exposed film. I tried to shift my worry to those potentially getting ruined.

A long dimly lit corridor was to the right of the X-ray machines. An attractive blonde woman in a Japan Airlines uniform emerged from the hall with a demeanor much like a Soviet Army drill instructor. She rapidly spoke Japanese, Russian, and then English. She seemed to know who James was as she gathered up the diplomatic group.

"There is a break in the snowstorm, and we must get this flight out of Moscow quickly," she said to James.

"Stay close to me and the other diplomats because we always get on the plane first," James muttered in my ear.

I was now absorbed into the diplomat group, and we were all quickly escorted down the dimly lit passageway, then aboard the Japan Airlines, Boeing 707 and directed to take seats in a larger than normal First Class section.

A few minutes later, the other passengers were loaded. The usual safety precautions were rapidly spoken in Russian, French, English, and Japanese. The Boeing 707 then taxied what seemed a short distance, stopped, revved its four engines, released its brakes with a jerk, accelerated with a roar much louder than usual, and this large jet was quickly airborne.

I could occasionally see Moscow city lights receding through breaks in the snow clouds. I felt my anxiety draining away and slumped into a deep sleep.

I was awakened by the stewardess with a moist hot towel. At that point, I remembered that in a few hours I would be out of the territory of the USSR and most importantly, I had *not* been searched because, **by international agreement, diplomats are not searched**! Fate or friends had acted to save me from the worst case scenario I'd been dreading since receiving the Speranski documents.

I was seated next to a diplomat from a Soviet Bloc country who was a former ambassador to the US. He knew I was from the US.

"Are you aware of what was happening in Washington, DC that was being called the 'Saturday Night Massacre'?" he asked.

"No," I said. "It's been impossible to get any news from outside the USSR."

The diplomat then described President Nixon's attempts to halt the Watergate investigation and how he had fired several members of his administration who had refused to fire the

Watergate Special Prosecutor.

I was skeptical of the validity of such an outrageous story especially from a "communist." I questioned the diplomat's source of information—surely, he shouldn't be trusting *Pravda* on such a story.

"I don't read *Pravda*—a 'terrible newspaper,'" he replied. "This story came from American newspapers such as the *Washington Post, New York Times, Chicago Tribune,* and *Los Angeles Times*. At my embassy, we get them all." His next statement was truly chilling.

"Young man, you will be very lucky when you return home, if your President Nixon has not ordered tanks onto the streets of Washington, DC."

In Japan, my visit to the University of Tokyo was shorter than originally planned due to the snowstorm in Moscow and my delayed departure. I was invited to a United Nations reception that involved the Club of Rome. There were Soviets at the reception, and I was uncomfortable I might say something bringing unwanted questions of me. I claimed to be feeling ill, excused myself, and went back to the hotel where I tried to settle down and be ready to board my flight to San Francisco where I would clear customs and then fly to Los Angeles to meet my wife and children on 31 October.

Return to JPL Pasadena

Early my first morning home, after a month away, a phone call came from Dr. Pickering's office. I was asked if I had anything for the Laboratory Director, and I replied yes and then "asked" to come to the director's office as soon as possible.

As I entered Dr. Pickering's office, Deputy Laboratory Director, General C. H. Terhune, was nearest the door and reached for the envelope as Dr. Pickering watched.

"What's going on?" I asked.

"Thank you and you may leave now," was the general's only answer.

Only four years earlier, I had had been a commissioned officer Lieutenant Junior Grade, (officer grade O-2) and now, in the presence of a former three-star Air Force general (officer grade O-9) who had spent his career giving orders and with a real voice of authority, I understood that the phrase "you may leave now" meant I was not going to be told anything.

Dr. Pickering stared at me for a moment, then in his soft-spoken New Zealand accent, said, "Thank you very much." I assumed the documents I had managed to get out of the USSR were soon to be communicated to the US Intelligence Community.

No Discussion of What Happened

October 1973

It became apparent to me that the Pickering and Terhune strategy regarding me and the Speranski documents would become, "No one discloses what actually happened in October 1973, and there will be no record or private discussion that such a decision ever existed."

Despite a couple of opportunities when Pickering and I *could* have had a private conversation, he would not discuss anything related to Speranski. This decision was likely the safest for all concerned and has persisted for more than four decades. I have decided that it is important to present these events now, in which I was peripherally involved, because **the world needs to understand that confrontations between nuclear weapons armed adversaries can quickly degenerate into an out of control calamity.**

An example occurred on the Mediterranean Sea in October 1973, when one of the sixty vessels of the US Navy 6th Fleet performed a routine calibration of its surface-to-surface missile-fire-control-radar system. The outgoing radar beam has a relatively wide angle of illumination and accidentally triggered a radar-threat-warning-receiver on one of the ninety-six Soviet ships of the Soviet 5th *Eskadra*. That Soviet ship responded by activating its missile-fire-control-radar system which cascaded into essentially all of the combatant vessels of two modern naval fleets prepared to fire at each other. It was a testament to the professionalism of both the US and Soviet fleets that World War III was not ignited by those accidental events.

You Were Perfect

By 1992, I was a professor in the Aerospace Engineering Sciences Department at the University of Colorado, Boulder involved in teaching and research. Because of my academic engineering position and a prior advisory role to the US Space Command, I was asked to be a technology risk assessment advisor to the FBI in Denver—a task which I accepted.

In a casual seeming meeting, while walking and talking along Boulder Creek with the FBI Special Agent and a member of the US intelligence community, Clandestine Services, I was asked to relate my 1973 USSR experience.

I was told by these government officials that they had never heard of anyone getting away with what I had done. I complained that I had had no training, having never been to the CIA's "Farm," the storied training facility of the Clandestine Service officers. Beyond that, I'd had no safe house, nor contacts, not even a phone number to call. I had seemed to be completely alone in the entire matter.

The reaction from the Bureau and the Agency regarding those events was summed up in the statement, "You were perfect." I was told that neither US entity had had any part in setting these events into motion. It had been strictly a decision on the part of Soviet citizens.

"There was no record of you being involved in any

clandestine services; you were really the scientist that you purported to be; you did not know about any ongoing sensitive activities in the USSR, and if the KGB had arrested and interrogated you, you could not have revealed any US or allied country operations."

As I would learn from Dr. Davies about 40 years after my USSR trip, if I had received a CIA briefing prior to my trip, the Soviets had the means to quickly know that such a briefing had occurred. Davies had refused to be briefed, although he'd agreed to be debriefed after his trip. Davies' understanding was that if he had been briefed prior to his trip, he would have been regarded as a US spy—arrested on entry into the USSR. I was not approached to be briefed by the Agency.

"What would have happened to me if the KGB had actually arrested me?" I asked the FBI Special Agent.

"Six months in Lubyanka—tops…and we would've traded you for one of theirs," he answered. (Lubyanka is the KGB prison in Moscow.) I did not regard this answer a comforting response.

Closing Thoughts

In May 1971, my first wife and I became foster parents for Nguyen Thi Bong, a Viet Nam War injured child who had sustained wounds from M-16 rifle fire and hand grenade shrapnel. My home was Bong's eighth US foster home in the three years she had been in the US for reconstructive surgeries.

By 1977, I was a single father raising an adopted son, Michael, and Bong. Then in 1981, by means of a single-parent adoption, she became Bong Thi MacDoran and, by a complex process, became a US Citizen. Both Michael and Bong became successful adults, thanks, in part, to my second wife, Judy, helping to fund two university educations.

A particularly poignant event for me involving Bong happened at a back-to-school elementary musical performance, just prior to my trip to the USSR. Bong was in the front row as they sang "Let there be peace on earth/ And let it begin with me."

In October 1973, Soviets, about my age, conducted their own vetting of me and wanted to know about my home life, likely to decide if I could be trusted. I told them about raising an adopted son and a war-injured girl, and that I had been through several reconstructive surgeries with her. Bong would eventually endure fifty-three reconstructive procedures. (All of these surgeries and hospitalizations were donated services.)

When Bong was five years old, she told me, in a slow and

halting voice, what seemed to be the story of when she got hurt. I had been told by a child psychiatrist that I had to keep Bong talking if she ever began telling about how she got hurt, so I said over and over, "And then what happened, Bong?"

She described seeing her mother dying and described what had happened to her own face—probably caused by grenade shrapnel. It was the most painful instruction I ever had to carry out. I was later warned by a psychotherapist that any person who had experienced what this child had endured would, at some time, experience a "major psychotic-break."

In December 2013, at the age of forty-seven, Bong committed suicide. My wife, Judy, observed that the demons of war had finally taken her away. Bong, to me, lived a life of bravery. She endured challenges that even as a young child helped me understand I had to do what I could to avoid a global war, which would inflict suffering beyond any ability to describe especially to non-combatants. So, Bong may have contributed to avoidance of a global nuclear war, and her school choir lyrics will always be special to me:

"Let there be peace on earth/ And let it begin with me."

Dr. Pickering and General Terhune, knew about the little war-injured girl living in my home which would make me a more likely candidate to be trusted by the Soviet dissidents. I now believe I was selected to be the courier from the first planning of how the dissidents could communicate their intent to turn against their government. Dr. Pickering and Dr. Davies became the targets to draw the KGB counter-intelligence away from me. I am endlessly grateful for the involvement of the Soviet dissidents in Baku, Moscow, and Leningrad, the diplomats from the US Embassy in Turkey; and James, the US academic; and the former Dutch general who were part of the Club of Rome who made possible my uneventful exit from the USSR.

To the Next Generation

Many young people are deterred from the study of science and engineering because they feel those topics are too hard and/or boring, and besides they would rather study things that help society. I hope my story may help them understand that the study of science and engineering can contribute in societal ways more important than they could possibly imagine.

Appendix I

Nuclear Weapons Reports

October 1973 E.P. Wilson was again being investigated by his employer (the Office of Naval Intelligence—ONI) for the same situation that had occurred earlier with the CIA: E.P. Wilson's amassing of tens of millions of dollars in assets and cash which he regarded as his personal property. Wilson feared the eminent termination of his ONI contract. To halt any such termination, he devised a scheme to prove his personal worth to the US Intelligence Community—in other words, Dr. Henry Kissinger. Wilson would exploit his prior relationship with Kissinger involving interactions with the People's Republic of China. During the China involvement, Wilson used the NSA cryptographic ROGER communications equipment some of which he had retained. He needed to report a huge intelligence finding related to this Mid-East War, such as developing proof that the Soviets were shipping nuclear warheads for Scud missiles by way of the Black Sea to Egypt that would then be expected to target Israel.

However, achieving such an intelligence coup posed a significant challenge. How to get close enough to the Soviet freighters to acquire cooling water discharge samples (used to manage the heat buildup associated with nuclear weapons in transport).

Nuclear materials generate heat that must be managed by a cooling system which in ship transport involves sea water intake and discharge. The seawater discharge can be expected to exhibit some level of nuclear contamination which can be detected with proper equipment.

Soviet freighters were traversing the Black Sea heading toward the Mediterranean Sea on their way to Egypt as I had witnessed on 2 October at Istanbul. If nuclear materials were present aboard these freighters, the cooling water discharge would be expected to contain trace amounts of radioactive material, Cesium 137, for example.

Wilson's scheme for getting close enough to the Soviet freighters to acquire water samples was quite ingenious. With ONI funds, he obtained an expensive high-powered pleasure boat and arranged to have several attractive women in bathing suits onboard waving at the Soviet sailors, making it seem that flirting was the only reason for their presence.

On approximately 22 October, Wilson with a couple of crew members and the young women cruised round and round the Soviet freighter *Mezhdurechensk* bound for Alexandria, Egypt, while water samples were surreptitiously acquired in close proximity to the vessel.

E.P. Wilson needed quick results rather than waiting for analysis by the US Naval Research Laboratory—the original plan. Thus, he likely performed his own technical analysis of the acquired samples. Note that Wilson's educational background was a BA degree in psychology; he had no formal education in nuclear physics. Based upon his personal judgment, he concluded that nuclear warheads were being transported by the Soviet freighter, *Mezhdurechensk.*

On 24 October, using the ROGER Channel, Wilson reported to Kissinger that nuclear weapons were on the Soviet freighter bound for Egypt.

On 25 October, at the forceful insistence of Kissinger and Haig, the US elevated its status to DEFCON 3, establishing a global alert against possible Soviet threats to US interests. The reaction in Israel to this DEFCON 3 escalation was to arm its nuclear weapons for a second time during this Yom Kippur War.

These events constituted a significant escalation and brought the threat that this 1973 war could become a nuclear conflict— precursor to WW3. US/Israel and USSR/Egypt/Syria are the two major factions involved either in direct military conflict or, as is the case of the US and USSR, are close to direct shooting engagements that could escalate into nuclear weapon exchanges.

There is no trusted third party (e.g., United Nations) that could be called upon in October 1973 to quickly perform an inspection of Soviet shipments to assure no nuclear warheads were being introduced into the conflict. (To this day, Israel will neither confirm nor deny possession of any nuclear weapons and would never acquiesce to on-site inspections.)

In the meantime, the Soviet dissidents had information from KGB sources (monitoring the presumed secure ROGER channel communications to the White House). The dissidents were aware that E.P. Wilson's report to Kissinger about detecting nuclear warheads was false since they knew that the Soviets had not supplied any nuclear warheads. The dissidents also knew this situation as extremely destabilizing. They needed a way to block anything from being offloaded from the freighter because any off-loaded cargo would be immediately suspect as being involved with the 24 October report of nuclear warheads.

Recall that the Soviet cruise ship I was aboard, the *M/S Armenia,* had sailed through the same zone of the Black Sea and at about the same time interval as the *Mezhdurechensk.* The cruise ship *M/S Armenia* cancelled its scheduled port-call because of an outbreak of cholera within the zone around the Port of Varna, Bulgaria. All that the dissidents needed to do was to create the fear that cargo or food and or drinking water might have been contaminated because of its proximity with the Port of Varna, Bulgaria. The possibility of a cholera outbreak is a powerful fear to any seaport and especially where military forces are involved. Several days to weeks of inspection or prophylaxes (measures taken to maintain health and prevent the spread of disease) would have been involved prior to any cargo off-loading.

In addition to the E.P. Wilson report, another suspicion of nuclear weapons in this Mid East War became a factor when an article in *Aviation Week and Space Technology,* a highly respected trade publication, reported the following:

Aviation Week and Space Technology, November 5, 1973, page 12

SOVIETS POISE THREE-FRONT GLOBAL DRIVE

Nuclear warheads to Egypt to force an Arab-oriented peace pact in the Middle East. Two brigades of Soviet Scud surface-to-surface missiles, each equipped with a nuclear warhead, are now in position east of Cairo poised to strike Tel Aviv and other Israeli population centers (aw&st Oct 22, p. 14). The single-stage storage-propellant Scuds, which remain under Russian control, were shipped from Soviet Black Sea port on Sept. 12, almost a month before the Oct. 6 outbreak of the latest fighting in the Middle East.

The publication date was November 5, 1973. In order to be available at press time, the article had to have been vetted and prepared some days earlier, possibly a mere few days after the Wilson report to Kissinger on 24 October 1973 leading to the DEFCON 3 declaration.

The Aviation Week nuclear warheads story reported two brigades of troops to staff the Scud missiles. This implied the presence of perhaps 4,000 troops and specialized ground equipment for the storage and loading of nuclear warheads that could be detected with spy satellites or spy plane over-flights.

The fact that the Soviet freighter *Mezhdurechensk* remained unloaded and that two missile brigades were not detected was confirmed by a combination of US spy satellites surveillance and SR-71 Black Bird aircraft photo reconnaissance over-flights.

The following is a concise summary: "There is no reliable information that nuclear weapons of any sort have ever been introduced into Egypt by the Soviets," W.B. Quandt, Rand Corporation, May 1976. See References.

I delivered the Speranski *bona fide* documents to Pickering and Terhune on 31 October, so by 5 November, the Soviet dissidents would have been in contact with elements of the US government, initiated by Dr. Pickering and General Terhune. The Pickering/Terhune channels were within the DoD, CIA, State Department and certain Committees of the US Congress, where the dissidents had an opportunity to convince US high level officials (outside the White House then in Watergate disarray) that Soviet nuclear weapons had never been introduced into Arab countries nor placed in control of Arab military forces. Only the US had the credibility to have the Israelis stand-down from a nuclear strike posture against the Yom Kippur War attackers. Had Israel launched its nuclear forces, the Soviet Union was likely to be an early target because of Israel's anger over the Soviets having armed the Arabs with modern weapons that precipitated the Yom Kippur War on the 6th of October 1973.

On the Mediterranean Sea, the Soviet Navy 5th *Eskadra* persisted in their attack formations against the US 6th Fleet carriers into early November 1973. By mid-November, the US Navy 6th Fleet was taken off alert and returned to a training status.

The world nearly cascaded into what Kissinger described as the "Annihilation of Humanity." The recipe that nearly had this result:

the USSR desire for expanded influence in the Middle East, the personal greed of a rogue CIA operator, the Nixon White House devotion to halting the Watergate scandal, and the ambitions of Dr. Kissinger and General Haig.

The "Annihilation of Humanity" was avoided by the actions of decent people from several countries with diverse personal backgrounds who were quite unlikely to ever meet under other circumstances.

For me, this became quite an unanticipated adventure initiated by Dr. William H. Pickering and General Charles H. Terhune. They believed I could—without prior knowledge or training— accomplish the task of being the courier for documents that were essential to establishing a back channel to the Soviet dissidents. Those documents could have been the cause of my death. The start of the Yom Kippur War during my trip into the USSR had been completely unexpected by Pickering and Terhune, and that greatly complicated every aspect of establishing the back channel. Most incredible, all of this happened completely out of the consciousness of the vast majority of the American population who were oblivious to the vast dangers engulfing the whole of humanity.

Appendix II

The Valery Plame Affair

Many years after the October 1973 events, a Washington Post story by Robert Novak in 2003, publically identified Valerie Plame Wilson as a covert CIA operative working on counter-proliferation of nuclear weapons. Such information disclosure to Robert Novak originated from within the White House and became a large scandal that necessitated that President George W. Bush commute the prison sentence of Scooter Libby, a senior staff member in the office of Vice President Dick Cheney.

This Robert Novak disclosure caused me to recall my own situation in 1973 and what could have happened to me and my family if my involvement with dissident Soviets had been disclosed. This kind of leak could have triggered serious risks for me from both the KGB operatives in the US and perhaps even the US intelligence community at home. The KGB would have been motivated to learn the identity of the Soviet dissidents in order to halt the back channel information to the US, and probably would have killed the dissidents and their families.

In a perverse looking-glass scenario, a simultaneous negative reaction from a CIA rogue element could have been motivated to arrange a "fatal accident" for me—to avoid the exposure of the dissidents and, thereby, destroy the CIA back channel into high levels of the Soviet government. In either scenario, the operatives (either KGB or CIA) might have targeted my family in order to gain control over me. The fact that I attained the research and development career I had wanted is perhaps due to international elements. I'm obviously glad things worked as they did…and that the world did not experience what Kissinger termed "The Annihilation of Humanity."

Acknowledgements

Judy Kay MacDoran, my best friend and wife of thirty-three years—for tolerance (AKA, occasional return trips for me to patience and understanding conducted by an intelligent woman) and for being a wonderful mom to my two adopted children and to our son, McKinley, a delightful addition to our lives as older parents.

Ariele M. Huff, my writing coach, editor of this project, and friend. Trust me, studying Physics and Electrical Engineering does not equip one to write in a manner that people willingly choose to read as entertainment.

Edward M. Gamez: my mother's father, mentor to me beginning at age seven who helped me assemble my first crystal radio receiver, and a 32rd Degree Mason who made sure I joined the Order of DeMolay, where I (pretty much) learned to function properly in social environments because he likely saw I was on the path to becoming, what is now described as, a high-functioning autistic.

Over the decades, there were several surgeons involved with Bong's reconstructive surgeries. However, based upon my personal years of raising Bong, a very special thanks goes to Dr. Richard Grossman (d. 2014), Sherman Oaks, California, and Dr. Elliott H. Rose, New York City. These surgeons were/are men of enormous skill and compassion. They also recruited others in the medical community to donate assistance to Bong that she might have as normal a life as was humanly possible.

Harry Schultheis: the first professional engineer I ever met, an amateur radio operator, father of my best grade school friend who taught us how to build things that actually worked and whose only daughter became my first wife.

Charles McClure, Reseda High School, my trigonometry teacher and former WW II bomber pilot whose class problems often involved navigating a B-24 bomber to places such as the Nazi controlled Ploiesti Oil Fields, one of the deadliest repeatedly bombed targets of WW II.

Dr. Eugene Nutter, my supervisor at Atomics International, where I worked my first year after high school graduation. He was a physicist and seemed to know many things beyond his own field of science—and I wanted to be that too. So, when I started college full-time and had to declare a major, I wrote Physics.

Dr. Richard Davies, who flew nearly seventy combat missions into Europe during WW II with the 8th Air Force as a navigator. He returned to Caltech after the war to do a PhD in Physics and I met him at JPL in 1970; in 1973, he was selected for surveillance by KGB counter-intelligence which helped me depart the USSR without being searched, and now, at age ninety-three, he remains a good friend.

NASA and the American taxpayers for funding Caltech/JPL Project ARIES that provided the basis upon which I was in the USSR during these difficult Cold War events: JPL managers Dr. Don Rea and Bill Newberry, Science Office; Dr. Nick Renzetti, Deep Space Network; Dr. Bill Melbourne, Section Manager; Don Trask, Group Supervisor; the ARIES technical team, Dr. George Resch, Dr. Art Neill, Dr. Henry Fliegel, Dr. Jack Fanselow, Dr. Brooks Thomas, Dr. Jim Williams, Dr. Kwok Ong, Lyle Skjerve, Don Spitzmesser, Leroy Tanita, Bob Miller, Dave Morabito, Carol Steinberg, Adrianna Ocampo, Dorothe Horttor, Bob Neustadt, Ben Johnson, Steve Paine, and Steve DiNardo; Caltech Radio Astronomy Professors Marshall Cohen, Alan Moffett, Dr. Dave Rogstad, and Dr. Marty Ewing; Caltech Seismological Laboratory, Dr. James Whitcomb; NASA Headquarters advocates for Project ARIES, Dr. Ben Milwitsky, Frank Williams, and Dr. Tom Fischetti.

Clear Image Photo, Everett, Washington, for the digital restoration of forty-three-year-old small format film images–thank you, Charles.

About the Author

Pete MacDoran holds degrees in physics (BS, California State University, Northridge, '64) and electrical engineering (MS, University of California, Santa Barbara, '66). He served to lieutenant (junior grade) in the National Oceanographic and Atmospheric Administration (NOAA), Commissioned Officer Corps with assignments in space geodesy and shipboard oceanography. For thirteen years, he was at the NASA/Caltech, Jet Propulsion Laboratory, where he was awarded both NASA medals—Exceptional Scientific Achievement and then Exceptional Engineering Achievement—and became the first person in NASA history to have been the recipient of both medals. He joined the George H. Born Center for Astrodynamics Research / Aerospace Engineering Sciences faculty at the University of Colorado, Boulder where he developed the first undergraduate teaching laboratory for GPS technology. With CU graduate students and wife, Judy, CyberLocator, Inc., was formed to commercialize unconventional methods for positioning, navigation, and timing, and location-based authentication cyber security which was awarded a US Patent, subsequently sold to a major US corporation. He has consulted on commercial and governmental topics as well as space technology litigation matters.

Edited by Ariele M. Huff

Cover art by Judy K. MacDoran

References

The Samson Option, Israel's Nuclear Arsenal and American Foreign Policy, by Seymour M. Hersh, Random House, New York, August 1991

Soviet Policy in the October 1973 War, William B. Quandt. A report prepared for the Office of the Assistant Secretary of Defense/International Security Affairs, Rand, R-1864-ISA, May 1976

Kissinger by Marvin Kalb and Bernard Kalb, Little, Brown and Company, Boston, 1974

Prelude to Terror, Edwin P. Wilson and the Legacy of America's Private Intelligence Network, Joseph J. Trento, Carroll & Graf Publishers, New York, 2005

Edwin P. Wilson, gunrunner and manager of CIA front companies, died on September 10th, aged 84, The Economist, Sep 29th 2012, http://www.economist.com/node/21563687

Edwin Wilson: The CIA's Great Gatsby, by Edward Jay Epstein, *PARADE*, Sep 18th 1993, http://www.edwardjayepstein.com/archived/edwin/print_htm

Legacy of Ashes—The History of the CIA, by Tim Weiner, Double Day, New York, 2007

Manhunt, The Dramatic Pursuit of a CIA Agent Turned Terrorist, ibooks, distributed by Simon and Schuster, New York, 2002

The National Security Archive, The October War and U.S. Policy, William Burr, editor, 10/7/2003

A Tale Of Two Fleets—A Russian Perspective on the 1973 Naval Standoff in the Mediterranean, by Lyle J. Goldstein and Yuri M. Zhukov, Yom Kippur War—time line—Naval War College Review—ADA42249.pdf, Spring 2004, Vol. LVII, No. 2 and October 2003 Issue of Navy League

Yom Kippur: Israel's 1973 nuclear alert, by Richard Sale, UPI Terrorism Correspondent, September 16, 2002

1973 DEFCON 3 alert, Boeing B-52Ds at Guam's Air Force Base were loaded with nuclear weapons. http://www.airspacemag.com/military-aviation/go-defcon-3-180949493/#ixzz2tznjtCig

Nixon and Kissinger—Partners in Power, by Robert Dallek, Harper Collins Publishers, 2007

William Pickering: Space Explorer (1910-2004), Notable American Unitarians, 1936-1961, Edited by Herbert F. Vetter, Harvard Square Library, Cambridge, Massachusetts 2007

PATRIOTS—The Vietnam War Remembered From All Sides— Bong MacDoran, interview by University of Massachusetts, historian, Christian G. Appy, pps 522-526, Penguin Books, 2003

NBC TODAY SHOW, Bong MacDoran interview by Katie Couric, November 23, 1995

Pete MacDoran in Leningrad, October 1973

—

Soviet Cruiser *Aurora*, whose blank cannon blast signaled the beginning of the Bolshevik Revolution of October 1917 that gave rise to the Union of Soviet Socialist Republics, the USSR

—

THEY CHOSE HIM TO STOP A NUCLEAR WAR.

Made in the USA
San Bernardino, CA
17 June 2016